Praise for *Whe*

"Knowing Carol for years, I had expected ... manuscript that it would be a good read. I was wrong. It is outstanding! Anyone facing any adversity, great or small, needs to read this. If you love real and helpful seasoned with a dose of humor, you will love this book. I'll predict once you read it, you'll be getting extra copies to give to friends – and get ready for a beneficial adjustment to your perspective on life."
—— Randy Pope, Founding Pastor, Perimeter Church

"At a time in her life when Carol could have easily been downcast, she chose to focus her gaze on her Heavenly Father. You will be encouraged by her journey through cancer as you face your own trials in life."
—— Dr. Amelia B. Zelnak, M.D., M. SC. Oncologist

Carol's poignant and vulnerable account of her journey resonates with all of us ... We are all in need of God's embrace, instruction, guidance and promise that He will walk with us through our trials. I love her humor! But I also am moved by her use of hymns and Bible verses which speak to us in times of despair and disquietude.
—— Jane Dausner, Palliative Care Social Worker

When Things Go Sideways

ALSO BY CAROL G. FREY

Have You Considered Cooking?

The Grits Shall Rise Again!

The Best Kids Party Book

When Things Go Sideways

A devotional of God's grace in times
when we get what we don't want

Carol G. Frey

ISBN-13:9781690828006

Cover photograph by John Westrock

All scripture in this book is English Standard Version.

All hymns in this book are public domain.
To access a playlist of these hymns go to
www.Facebook.com/carolfreyauthor

To my husband Paul who faithfully and untiringly walked with
me on my journey through cancer.

The Lord is good, a stronghold in the day of trouble; he knows
those who take refuge in him.

NAHUM 1:7

INTRODUCTION

I was minding my own business. Then out of the blue on my wedding anniversary I received a diagnosis of triple negative breast cancer. Not my idea of a fun anniversary surprise. Surprise … yes; fun … not so much. The following year took me through a maze of cancer treatments and their aftermath. And from beginning to end God was there … ever-faithful, ever-present, ever a stronghold. God was there when things went sideways.

TABLE OF CONTENTS

1
ORNERY

I am the door. If anyone enters by me, he will be saved and will
go in and out and find pasture. The thief comes only to steal
and kill and destroy. I came that they may have life
and have it abundantly.

JOHN 10:9-10

I was ornery. After listening to a monotone message from the breast imaging center and hanging up the phone, I scoffed; rolled my eyes even. They always make me come back and it's always for no good reason, I grumbled knowingly to my ever-patient husband.

I dutifully returned to the imaging center as I always do, taking my time about making the appointment since I knew it would be routine nothingness as it had been in the past. Not this time.

———————

It is a trip I never wanted to go on and now it is a trip I never would have missed.

———————

This time called for another appointment, an even more invasive procedure, with extra time afterward to mull over my previous know-it-all attitude. I figured it's not so bad to be confident and sure of yourself by virtue of being empirically informed; unless you're wrong. Hate when that happens. The good news is that there *is* someone who knows beyond empirically, always, every time and without fail. It just doesn't happen to be me.

And so my journey began. It was new and also old. Many had gone along this path before, but it was a new one for me and maybe it is for you. It was a trip of don't be so sure, don't rush ahead, but don't worry. It was my journey of being carried instead of carrying, of waiting instead of rushing ahead, of being a patient patient. None of these conditions were chosen by me but they were chosen for me by my wise and wonderful Heavenly Father. This entire journey was brought to me carefully, graciously and lovingly by him. It is a trip I never wanted to go on and now it is a trip I never would have missed.

Count on this ...

> *The Lord is my shepherd; I shall not want. He makes me lie down in green pastures. He leads me beside still waters. He restores my soul. He leads me in paths of righteousness, for his name's sake. Even though I walk through the valley of the shadow of death, I will fear no evil; for you are with me; your rod and your staff, they comfort me. You prepare a table before me in the presence of my enemies; you anoint my head with oil; my cup overflows. Surely goodness and mercy shall follow me all the days of my life, and I shall dwell in the house of the Lord forever.*
> PSALM 23

HOW FIRM A FOUNDATION

How firm a foundation, ye saints of the Lord,
is laid for your faith in His excellent Word!
What more can He say than to you He hath said,
to you who for refuge to Jesus have fled?

Fear not, I am with thee; O be not dismayed,
for I am thy God and will still give thee aid.
I'll strengthen thee, help thee, and cause thee to stand,
upheld by My righteous, omnipotent hand.

When through the deep waters I call thee to go,
the rivers of sorrow shall not overflow;
for I will be with thee, thy troubles to bless,
and sanctify to thee thy deepest distress.

When through fiery trials thy pathway shall lie,
My grace, all-sufficient, shall be thy supply.
The flame shall not hurt thee; I only design
thy dross to consume, and thy gold to refine.

The soul that on Jesus hath leaned for repose
I will not, I will not desert to its foes;
that soul, though all hell should endeavor to shake,
I'll never, no never, no never forsake!

George Keith and R. Keen (1787)

2
SORRY TO HAVE TO TELL YOU

*For I know the plans I have for you, declares the Lord, plans
for welfare and not for evil, to give you a future and a hope.*

JEREMIAH 29:11

"I'm sorry to have to tell you …" Not half as sorry as I am, I mentally snapped back as the bad news rolled out of the phone and into my ear. "The report shows that you have a malignancy in your right breast." I had already been told I had a spot. A spot I could digest. Spots come and go. Maybe it was nothing. But a malignancy? No thank you.

Eighty percent. Eighty percent was the chance that I had of not having cancer. The two lumps that were found were eighty percent more likely to be non-malignant than malignant. Great odds, but not my odds. I was among the twenty percent. The twenty percent that hung up the phone with a dazed look on their face. The twenty percent that quietly digested this new, unwanted and life-altering information.

God loves you and has a wonderful plan for your life, the old chant whispered to me. By whose definition was this a wonderful plan? Not mine. Not my idea of a good time. But then I am not the definer, so maybe my definitions need to change. This may not have been my definition of a good time, but it was God's definition of his best for me.

You may not enjoy every step of the way through your greatest trials, but you will always be in good hands. You will be carried by the One who watches over you, looks after you and bathes you in his grace. The One who has a wonderful plan for your life.

———————

You will be carried by the One who watches over you, looks after you and bathes you in his grace. The One who has a wonderful plan for your life.

———————

Hear the truth from God's word...

O God, you are my God; earnestly I seek you; my soul thirsts for you; my flesh faints for you, as in a dry and weary land where there is no water. So I have looked upon you in the sanctuary, beholding your power and glory. Because your steadfast love is better than life, my lips will praise you. So I will bless you as long as I live; in your name I will lift up my hands. My soul will be satisfied as with fat and rich food and my mouth will praise you with joyful lips, when I remember you upon my bed, and meditate on you in the watches of the night; for you have been my help, and in the shadow of your wings I will sing for joy. My soul clings to you; your right hand upholds me.

PSALM 63:1-8

HIS EYE IS ON THE SPARROW

Why should I feel discouraged?
Why should the shadows come?
Why should my heart be lonely
and long for heaven and home,
when Jesus is my portion?
My constant friend is he:
his eye is on the sparrow,
and I know he watches me;
his eye is on the sparrow,
and I know he watches me.

Refrain:
I sing because I'm happy,
I sing because I'm free,
for his eye is on the sparrow,
and I know he watches me.

"Let not your heart be troubled,"
his tender word I hear,
and resting on his goodness,
I lose my doubts and fears;
though by the path he leadeth
but one step I may see:
his eye is on the sparrow,
and I know he watches me;
his eye is on the sparrow,
and I know he watches me. [*Refrain*]

Civilla D. Martin (1905)

3
WHAT DID I DO TO DESERVE THIS?

but God shows his love for us in that while we were still
sinners, Christ died for us.

ROMANS 5:8

Did I deserve to get cancer? Interesting word 'deserve', to be worthy of. Cancer was not something I wanted to be worthy of. I'll pass. Did I get cancer because of my imperfections (sin)? I know I'm not perfect, but did I deserve that? Then my memory kicked in and I recalled a verse I memorized in college, "All have sinned and come short of the glory of God" (Romans 3:23). But still I ... again my memory kicked in. It's rough on you to keep remembering the truth of God's word when you're trying to feel sorry for yourself. "The wages of sin is death, but the gift of God is eternal life through Christ Jesus our Lord" (Romans 6:23). So I'm worthy to be dead forever because I'm sinful. Ouch! It's not that a particular sin of mine caused me to have an illness like cancer; but, since I am sinful and live in a fallen world where bad things happen, I 'deserve' to have cancer just as much as the next person. I could have asked, "Why me?" but I could also have asked, "Why not me?".

Inequitable, wonderful, unexplainable ... Jesus' love for us.

But Jesus, who is worthy to sit at God's right hand, is faultless and beyond reproach, and has not sinned once ever, was taken from his throne in heaven and put on earth to live; a complete downgrade. He didn't deserve that. Throughout his life he taught us the ways of righteousness and true love yet he was called by his Father to die an agonizing death on the cross. He took on every sin that you, I and everyone past, present and future invested in and took the insurmountable weight of them onto his guiltless shoulders. To the very depths of hell he carried those burdens. He didn't deserve that. And then up he rose from the depth of all depths to once and for all conquer sin. We didn't deserve that.

Did Jesus get what he deserved? No. He willingly took on what I deserved. Did I get what I deserve? No. I gratefully and joyfully take the grace that he afforded me. Inequitable, wonderful, unexplainable ... Jesus' love for us.

The truth is ...

> *For God so loved the world, that he gave his only Son, that whoever believes in him should not perish but have eternal life.*
> JOHN 3:16

See #1 in Afterwords page 105.

AND CAN IT BE

And can it be that I should gain
An int'rest in the Savior's blood?
Died He for me, who caused His pain—
For me, who Him to death pursued?
Amazing love! How can it be,
That Thou, my God, shouldst die for me?

Refrain:
Amazing love! How can it be,
That Thou, my God, shouldst die for me?

He left His Father's throne above—
So free, so infinite His grace—
Emptied Himself of all but love,
And bled for Adam's helpless race:
'Tis mercy all, immense and free,
For, O my God, it found out me! [*Refrain*]

Long my imprisoned spirit lay,
Fast bound in sin and nature's night;
Thine eye diffused a quick'ning ray—
I woke, the dungeon flamed with light;
My chains fell off, my heart was free,
I rose, went forth, and followed Thee. [*Refrain*]

No condemnation now I dread;
Jesus, and all in Him, is mine;
Alive in Him, my living Head,
And clothed in righteousness divine,
Bold I approach th' eternal throne,
And claim the crown, through Christ my own. [*Refrain*]

Charles Wesley (1738)

4
MISTAKE

Why are you cast down, O my soul, and why are you in turmoil
within me? Hope in God; for I shall again praise him,
my salvation and my God.

I couldn't wait to get to my doctor's appointment with my well thought out list of concerns. As soon as the breast care specialist came into the exam room and we said our hellos, I started streaming the questions. Could this be a mistake? Wouldn't it be ironic if we did all of this chemo and went to all of this trouble and the diagnosis turned out to be a mistake? Or what if the original diagnosis turned out to be wrong? Tests give false positives sometimes, maybe this time. Wouldn't it be silly to miss something like that? I felt hopeful.

I might have wondered about how things were
going to turn out, but I never needed to wonder
about God and his care for me.

I looked quizzically at my doctor, a faint smile at the corner of my mouth. She gazed at me with a mixture of warmth and resignation. We could do the tests all over again, but the results would be the same. They're conclusive she told me. As much disappointment as the answer gave me, I was glad for my wondering to stop.

13

Was I putting too much hope in the doctors, the assessments and the upcoming chemo? I was hopeful that the doctors would do their very best, that the treatment would work and that it would kill my cancer. And that was a good and worthwhile hope. I had put myself in the hands of these capable physicians and their treatments but my ultimate bottom-line hope lay in Jesus my Savior. I might have wondered about how things were going to turn out, but I never needed to wonder about God and his care for me. In him my hope is secure. In his hands I will never be disappointed. My focus needs to be up not out ... it's conclusive.

Put your hope in this ...

> *Blessed be the Lord, for he has wondrously shown his steadfast love to me when I was in a besieged city. I had said in my alarm, "I am cut off from your sight." But you heard the voice of my pleas for mercy when I cried to you for help. ... Be strong, and let your heart take courage, all you who wait for the Lord!*
> PSALM 31:21-22, 24

See #4 in Afterwords page 105.

MY HOPE IS BUILT ON NOTHING LESS

My hope is built on nothing less
than Jesus' blood and righteousness;
I dare not trust the sweetest frame,
but wholly lean on Jesus' name.

Refrain:
On Christ, the solid Rock, I stand;
all other ground is sinking sand,
all other ground is sinking sand.

When darkness veils His lovely face,
I rest on His unchanging grace;
in ev'ry high and stormy gale
my anchor holds within the veil.[*Refrain*]

His oath, His covenant, His blood
support me in the 'whelming flood;
when all around my soul gives way
He then is all my hope and stay.[*Refrain*]

When He shall come with trumpet sound,
O may I then in Him be found,
dressed in His righteousness alone,
faultless to stand before the throne. [*Refrain*]

Edward Mote (1834)

5
WESTWARD HO

If we say we have no sin, we deceive ourselves, and the truth is not in us. If we confess our sins, he is faithful and just to forgive us our sins and to cleanse us from all unrighteousness. If we say we have not sinned, we make him a liar, and his word is not in us.

1 JOHN 1:8-10

No way did I want to miss our trip out West for the birth of grandchild number seven. I begged and cajoled, some would say annoyed, the office staff at the breast care center to get the first round of tests and doctors visits in quickly so I could whisk away to my family and put cancer on the back burner for a minute. So, the office did its scheduling and I did my whisking. Then back home for three more rapid-fire doctors visits and *boom* ... chemo would begin. Our other western-dwelling family was due for a visit at our house the week following my return. So I asked the oncologist, very politely I might add, if we could start chemo after they'd left. Leaving little, as in no, room for discussion she said, "No we're starting next week." Okie dokie then, chemo it was. This lady is small but very convincing.

Just because we can't see something doesn't mean it's not there.

My cancer was caught early, so during the interim between initial diagnosis and the chemo I felt fine. It seemed surreal to feel completely well while knowing that there was something living inside

17

of me that would, if not eradicated, kill me. Then it hit me that the cancer was just like sin in my life. It can grow and fester while I continue on my oblivious way, feeling just fine. Or I might recognize my sin but choose to ignore it. Ignore-ance isn't bliss.

Just because we can't see something doesn't mean it's not there. We don't always see the root of our sin but the evidences are clear. We don't see God but the evidences of him are clear. We can't separate ourselves from our sin but God can. In fact, it's already been done by Jesus' work on the cross. So in the same way we put our illness in the hands of our doctors and their treatments, we can put our sin and ourselves in the hands of our Savior and God. It's the only solution.

For a fuller view …

> *For while we were still weak, at the right time Christ died for the ungodly. For one will scarcely die for a righteous person—though perhaps for a good person one would dare even to die but God shows his love for us in that while we were still sinners, Christ died for us. Since, therefore, we have now been justified by his blood, much more shall we be saved by him from the wrath of God. For if while we were enemies we were reconciled to God by the death of his Son, much more, now that we are reconciled, shall we be saved by his life. More than that, we also rejoice in God through our Lord Jesus Christ, through whom we have now received reconciliation.*
>
> ROMANS 5:6-11

NOTHING BUT THE BLOOD OF JESUS

What can wash away my sin?
Nothing but the blood of Jesus.
What can make me whole again?
Nothing but the blood of Jesus.

Refrain:
O precious is the flow
that makes me white as snow;
no other fount I know;
nothing but the blood of Jesus.

For my pardon this I see:
nothing but the blood of Jesus.
For my cleansing this my plea:
nothing but the blood of Jesus. [*Refrain*]

Nothing can for sin atone:
nothing but the blood of Jesus.
Naught of good that I have done:
nothing but the blood of Jesus. [*Refrain*]

This is all my hope and peace:
nothing but the blood of Jesus.
This is all my righteousness:
nothing but the blood of Jesus. [*Refrain*]

Robert Lowry (1876)

6
BUSY

We destroy arguments and every lofty opinion raised against
the knowledge of God, and take every thought captive
to obey Christ …

2 CORINTHIANS 10:5

Can't talk now, too busy. Just found out I have cancer so there's lots to do, appointments to make, a wig to buy… ah yes, buying a wig.

As soon as I found out I had cancer I jumped into action. One of those first actions was shopping for a wig. It's never hard for me to make a choice to go shopping. Entering a recommended wig shop I informed the lady that I had a big head. Having probably heard that before she said knowingly that she'd measure it, which she did and then pronounced, "You *do* have a big head!" Hum. When you fall into the big head category there aren't many wigs in your size. In this shop there were two. One was blonde and looked like it could have belonged to Dolly Parton; the other was very short and would have made me look like a pixie if someone close to six feet tall can look that way. They can't. Undaunted, I left the store and weeks later finally bought a wig online. Her name was Harriet. She looked okay on me according to what others said, but she was itchy and made me feel like I had an animal perched on my head. An animal that might decide to exit at the slightest provocation. So, Harriet and I got along best when she was on her stand in my closet and I was wearing a scarf.

God afforded me his heavenly hand brake called cancer to help me to stop, look and listen to him.

And so I busied myself. Busied myself with wig buying, appointment going, getting together with friends and doing any number of things, all the while avoiding the one thing God was calling me to do which was to stop. To quiet myself in him. To listen to that still small voice that goes unnoticed when we surround ourselves with so much noise.

God afforded me his heavenly hand brake called cancer to help me to stop, look and listen to him. Thank you Lord for that gift.

Prayer: Lord, please help me to stop my hurrying, to "Be still and know I am God" (Psalm 46:10a).

To look into your word, "All Scripture is breathed out by God and profitable for teaching, for reproof, for correction, and for training in righteousness" (2 Timothy 3:16).

And to listen to and follow after you, "My sheep hear my voice, and I know them, and they follow me" (John 10:27).

IN THE GARDEN

I come to the garden alone,
While the dew is still on the roses;
And the voice I hear, falling on my ear,
The Son of God discloses.

Refrain:
And He walks with me, and He talks with me,
And He tells me I am His own,
And the joy we share as we tarry there,
None other has ever known.

He speaks, and the sound of His voice
Is so sweet the birds hush their singing;
And the melody that He gave to me
Within my heart is ringing. [*Refrain*]

I'd stay in the garden with Him
Tho' the night around me be falling;
But He bids me go; thro' the voice of woe,
His voice to me is calling. [*Refrain*]

C. Austin Miles (1913)

7
CHEMO

Fear not, for I am with you; be not dismayed, for I am your
God; I will strengthen you, I will help you, I will uphold you
with my righteous right hand.

ISAIAH 41:10

My first day of chemo was a whirlwind. All I wanted to do was get through with it and get back home. It didn't seem ominous to me; I was too busy for ominous. My son and his family had arrived from Boise late the night before, and all I wanted to do was get back home and be with them and celebrate my husband's birthday. Happy birthday to Paul, your wife has cancer. Some birthday gifts are better than others. My daughter took time off of work to pick me up very early in the morning and drive through heavy traffic, the only kind available around here, and sat with me through those first long hours of chemo.

First a visit with my doctor and then on to the chemo room, a huge place with chairs for at least thirty people. How could they possibly need that many seats in this one hospital in a city as big as Atlanta, with multiple hospitals and cancer facilities? How many people are running around here with cancer? Well, most of them aren't exactly 'running around' as I soon found out while my daughter escorted my weak and dizzy self to the car.

I got home just in time to chat with everyone, tell them about my chemo, hug my grandchildren and then take a two-hour nap before birthday time. With the aid of many fine drugs to ward off some of the side effects of chemo, the visit with my family was wonderful. We watched fish swim at the local aquarium, watched our grandchildren swim (not at the aquarium) and cherished our time together which was punctuated by the baptism of our grandson, at our church and performed by our son from Boise, a pastor. The visit was good.

Many were there as I began my chemo journey. The treatments continued, each one becoming less palatable than the previous. And there was God, ever-present, ever-knowing, ever-keeping me. I knew that the results would be good no matter what, because my God is good no matter what.

———

I knew that the results would be good no matter what, because my God is good no matter what.

———

Read from God's word …

I will extol you, my God and King, and bless your name forever and ever. Every day I will bless you and praise your name forever and ever. Great is the Lord, and greatly to be praised, and his greatness is unsearchable. One generation shall commend your works to another, and shall declare your mighty acts. On the glorious splendor of your majesty, and on your wondrous works, I will meditate. They shall speak of the might of your awesome deeds, and I will declare your greatness. They shall pour forth the fame of your abundant goodness and shall sing aloud of your righteousness. The Lord is gracious and merciful, slow to anger and abounding in steadfast love. The Lord is good to all, and his mercy is over all that he has made. All your works shall give thanks to you, O Lord, and all your saints shall bless you!

PSALM 145:1-10

OH WORSHIP THE KING

O worship the King all-glorious above,
O gratefully sing his power and his love:
our shield and defender, the Ancient of Days,
pavilioned in splendor and girded with praise.

O tell of his might and sing of his grace,
whose robe is the light, whose canopy space.
His chariots of wrath the deep thunderclouds form,
and dark is his path on the wings of the storm.

Your bountiful care, what tongue can recite?
It breathes in the air, it shines in the light;
it streams from the hills, it descends to the plain,
and sweetly distills in the dew and the rain.

Frail children of dust, and feeble as frail,
in you do we trust, nor find you to fail.
Your mercies, how tender, how firm to the end,
our Maker, Defender, Redeemer, and Friend!

O measureless Might, unchangeable Love,
whom angels delight to worship above!
Your ransomed creation, with glory ablaze,
in true adoration shall sing to your praise!

Robert Grant (1833)

8
THE CHURCH

We give thanks to God always for all of you, constantly
mentioning you in our prayers, remembering before our
God and Father your work of faith and labor of love
and steadfastness of hope in our Lord Jesus Christ.

1 THESSALONIANS 1:2-3

I recognized the church maybe for the first time. I have been a part of the church for years, but this time I recognized it. It was brought to me by its people, the saints. I recognized not what I had been told since my youth but something even better, more divine. I had been told that the church is not a building, but it is the people. I realized that it's not just the people, but it is God in the form of his Spirit living and working through the people. When I picture God's Spirit moving, working, dwelling in the hearts of people over the entire globe, it seems glorious. It's indescribable, which is why I'll stop trying to describe it.

The church showed up.

But I won't stop saying that the church showed itself to me in ways I never dreamed of. People asked, "How can I help?" Over and over again they asked and I believe they meant it. Over and over again my response was, "You can pray." And they did. The church showed up with food and with Bible verse bookmarks handed to me by children with faces of pride and curiosity; and they prayed. They showed up with time spent and queries made;

and they prayed. They showed up in out-of-town places ... people I'd never met stopped me; and they prayed. They showed up and maybe even forgot to pray. The church showed up.

Hear more from God's word ...

> *And let us not grow weary of doing good, for in due season we will reap, if we do not give up. So then, as we have opportunity, let us do good to everyone, and especially to those who are of the household of faith.*
>
> GALATIANS 6:9-10

See #2 in Afterwords page 105.

FOR ALL THE SAINTS

For all the saints who from their labors rest,
who Thee by faith before the world confessed;
Thy name, O Jesus, be forever blest.
Alleluia, Alleluia!

Thou wast their Rock, their Fortress, and their Might;
Thou, Lord, their Captain in the well-fought fight;
Thou, in the darkness drear, their one true Light.
Alleluia, Alleluia!

O blest communion, fellowship divine!
We feebly struggle, they in glory shine;
yet all are one in Thee, for all are Thine.
Alleluia, Alleluia!

And when the strife is fierce, the warfare long,
steals on the ear the distant triumph song,
and hearts are brave again, and arms are strong.
Alleluia, Alleluia!

But when there breaks a yet more glorious day;
the saints triumphant rise in bright array;
the King of glory passes on His way.
Alleluia, Alleluia!

From earth's wide bounds, from ocean's farthest coast,
through gates of pearl streams in the countless host,
in praise of Father, Son, and Holy Ghost.
Alleluia, Alleluia!

William Walsham How (1864)

9
I'M STRUGGLING

The Lord bless you and keep you; The Lord make His face
shine upon you, And be gracious to you; The Lord lift up His
countenance upon you, And give you peace.

NUMBERS 6:24-26

She had designed a very fashionable princess costume for her-
self, made out of two rather large-ish blankets from the blanket
chest. Donned in this contraption along with clicky princess high
heels, Evie, my granddaughter, was slowly trying to make her way
across the room but her blanket garment kept tripping her up.
After several attempts to subjugate her outfit she stopped,
looked up in dismay and said, "I'm struggling." She was three. It
was funny. And being the helpful and compassionate grand-
mother that I am, I sat on the sofa and laughed. We all have our
roles.

God didn't make my struggles disappear but he
walked with me through them, by my side every
step of the way.

I struggled too, to navigate through my cancer. It weighed me
down. Even when I was feeling relatively normal my cancer was
still there just like my other struggles. But I praise God for his
great mercy to me. He didn't sit on the sofa and laugh at me for
trying to carry something that was clearly too heavy, something

I couldn't control. Instead he lifted my burdens and was at my side as I made my way through that hard time. God didn't make my struggles disappear, but he walked with me through them, beside me every step of the way. He stilled me in himself and rocked me in his arms so no matter how sick I was, I experienced comfort and peace. Not physical comfort but healing grace that only he can give. When I read the above verses (Numbers 6:24-26) for my own meditation I change the word *you* to *me* and watch my struggles subside.

For further meditation …

> *Praise the Lord! Praise the Lord, O my soul! I will praise the Lord as long as I live; I will sing praises to my God while I have my being. Put not your trust in princes, in a son of man, in whom there is no salvation. When his breath departs, he returns to the earth; on that very day his plans perish. Blessed is he whose help is the God of Jacob, whose hope is in the Lord his God, who made heaven and earth, the sea, and all that is in them, who keeps faith forever; who executes justice for the oppressed, who gives food to the hungry. The Lord sets the prisoner free; the Lord opens the eyes of the blind. The Lord lifts up those who are bowed down; the Lord loves the righteous. The Lord watches over the sojourners; he upholds the widow and the fatherless, but the way of the wicked he brings to ruin. The Lord will reign forever, your God, O Zion, to all generations. Praise the Lord!*

PSALM 146

IT IS WELL WITH MY SOUL

When peace like a river attendeth my way,
when sorrows like sea billows roll;
whatever my lot, thou hast taught me to say,
"It is well, it is well with my soul."

Refrain
It is well with my soul;
it is well, it is well with my soul.

Though Satan should buffet, though trials should come,
let this blest assurance control:
that Christ has regarded my helpless estate,
and has shed his own blood for my soul. [*Refrain*]

My sin oh, the bliss of this glorious thought!
my sin, not in part, but the whole,
is nailed to the cross, and I bear it no more;
praise the Lord, praise the Lord, O my soul! [*Refrain*]

O Lord, haste the day when my faith shall be sight,
the clouds be rolled back as a scroll;
the trump shall resound and the Lord shall descend;
even so, it is well with my soul. [*Refrain*]

Horatio G. Spafford (1873)

10
ANSWERING QUESTIONS

Wait for the Lord; be strong, and let your heart take courage;
wait for the Lord!

PSALM 27:14

I was asked twice in one week very detailed and personal questions about my cancer surgery, both times by people I did not have a close relationship with and once while one of them was standing beside her husband. I was taken aback both times. I have a very hard time deflecting direct questions that have an honest and specific answer, because I first and foremost want to be honest and truthful; except when I don't want to. I found myself forced into a situation in which I wanted to say, "Really? That's none of your business." But my thin film of good manners didn't allow for that. So I fumbled through both conversations finding neither of them to turn out well for either party involved. Some people need the courage to speak up. I needed the courage to shut up. Some question-answering options that I'm trying to learn are: 1. When called for, answer a question directly. I have that one down. 2. Saying "I'd rather not answer that." I don't have that one down. Or 3. Saying nothing. I sure don't have that one down. They're all okay. Just pray before responding. I don't have that one down either!

Lord, please help me to wait, quiet myself and rely on you.

As I pondered my experience I found myself thinking about the word 'fend'. They were left to fend for themselves. Or, I had to fend off the charging cockroach. (You had to be there.) I thought of the words offend and defend. In both of the situations above I felt like I needed to fend for myself. I can do that; sometimes, imperfectly, painfully and often awkwardly. But in the grand scheme of things God doesn't call me to do that. He knows I'm fallible. I'm the one who seems to forget that. He knows I need to rely on him. I desperately want to learn that. He is my ultimate defender.

Prayer: Lord, please help me to wait, quiet myself and rely on you.

God's word says …

> *This Book of the Law shall not depart from your mouth, but you shall meditate on it day and night, so that you may be careful to do according to all that is written in it. For then you will make your way prosperous, and then you will have good success. Have I not commanded you? Be strong and courageous. Do not be frightened, and do not be dismayed, for the Lord your God is with you wherever you go.*
>
> JOSHUA 1:8-9

I NEED THEE EVERY HOUR

I need thee every hour,
most gracious Lord;
no tender voice like thine
can peace afford.

Refrain:
I need thee, O I need thee;
every hour I need thee!
O bless me now, my Savior,
I come to thee.

I need thee every hour,
stay thou near by;
temptations lose their power
when thou art nigh. [*Refrain*]

I need thee every hour,
in joy or pain;
come quickly, and abide,
or life is vain. [*Refrain*]

I need thee every hour;
teach me thy will,
and thy rich promises
in me fulfill. [*Refrain*]

Annie Hawks and Robert Lowry (1872)

11
LONELY BUT NOT ALONE

For I am sure that neither death nor life, nor angels nor rulers,
nor things present nor things to come, nor powers, nor height nor
depth, nor anything else in all creation, will be able to separate
us from the love of God in Christ Jesus our Lord.

ROMANS 8:38-39

I felt alone. Hello, I was alone … that solves that mystery. Even so, I didn't always feel lonesome when I was by myself. Sometimes I felt relieved and sometimes I felt asleep, because I was asleep. But whenever loneliness set in, I sure didn't like the feeling. Not only did I dislike it, my perfectionist self didn't approve of it. I thought of feeling lonely as self-pity.

During my cancer I undeservingly found myself surrounded by people supporting me, helping me and praying for me. There were so many people just a phone call and a listening ear away. They were physical, available, heavenly-placed reminders of God's love and faithfulness to me. And even with all of that and all of them, I sometimes felt deserted. Go figure. Even while surrounded by empathy and God-sent love from so many, loneliness existed within me. Still does sometimes.

The people who were by my side as I walked through cancer were physical, available, heavenly-placed reminders of God's love and faithfulness to me.

But God understands. He understands my feelings of aloneness. He doesn't require me to pull myself up by my bootstraps, shake it off, get over it and move on. He who created me understands me more and better than anyone else. He turns away from my sinful behavior but he doesn't turn away from me.

He waits.

He is there.

He stills me, when I will be stilled.

He reminds me of himself, when I will be reminded.

He brings me to repentance with a gentle hand.

He holds me in his arms.

I am grateful.

Learn more good news ...

Therefore, as you received Christ Jesus the Lord, so walk in him, rooted and built up in him and established in the faith, just as you were taught, abounding in thanksgiving.

COLOSSIANS 2:6-7

COME THOU FOUNT OF EVERY BLESSING

Come thou fount of every blessing,
tune my heart to sing thy grace;
Streams of mercy never ceasing
call for songs of loudest praise.
Teach me some melodious sonnet
sung by flaming tongues above.
Praise the mount I'm fixed upon it
mount of thy redeeming love.

Here I raise my Ebenezer,
hither by thy help I come.
And I hope by thy good pleasure
safely to arrive at home.
Jesus sought me when a stranger
wandering from the fold of God.
He, to rescue me from danger
interposed His precious blood.

O to grace how great a debtor
daily I'm constrained to be!
Let thy goodness like a fetter,
bind my wandering heart to thee.
Prone to wander Lord I feel it,
prone to leave the God I love.
Here's my heart, O take and seal it,
seal it for thy courts above.

Robert Robinson (1785), Martin Maden (1760)

12
JOYFUL

For you shall go out in joy and be led forth in peace; the
mountains and the hills before you shall break forth into
singing, and all the trees of the field shall clap their hands.

ISAIAH 55:12

I like to have fun. Fun is for me. There it is, plain and simple. Having cancer is definitely not fun.

For some, the disease they carry may be life threatening, even life ending. In many cases fun is beyond consideration, even insulting to mention. So I will revert to saying I like to be joyful. But how could I be joyful with the noose of cancer hanging around my neck?

First of all, nobody said I needed to remain somber and morose during the whole process of battling a disease. Whew! The best news is, God doesn't require or even want that for me. Smiling and laughing are good. Proverbs 17:22 says, "A joyful heart is good medicine..." and when you have cancer you need all the good medicine you can get.

With God's Spirit living inside of me I had something to smile about, cancer or not.

I love the Broadway tune, *Put on a Happy Face*. The song is not theologically accurate in saying that gray skies are going to clear

45

up if you smile, but it sure doesn't hurt … to smile that is. It doesn't hurt the people around you either to see that face they love smiling back at them. I realize this sounds somewhat 'self-helpy' because it is. Try smiling sometimes … it won't crack your face. Inside the house or out, smile and make eye contact with people. You can even practice at home alone, like exercising, nobody has to see you do it.

With God's Spirit living inside of me I had something to smile about, cancer or not. Then and now I am filled with the joy of knowing that God has poured his grace over me again and again. He sent his Son to die in my place. He adopted me as his child and he guides me through the hardest of trials. He is here for me. He is here for you. It's enough to make you smile.

Read more from God's word …

> Oh come, let us sing to the Lord; let us make a joyful noise to the rock of our salvation! Let us come into his presence with thanksgiving; let us make a joyful noise to him with songs of praise! For the Lord is a great God, and a great King above all gods. In his hand are the depths of the earth; the heights of the mountains are his also. The sea is his, for he made it, and his hands formed the dry land. Oh come, let us worship and bow down; let us kneel before the Lord, our Maker! For he is our God, and we are the people of his pasture, and the sheep of his hand…
>
> PSALM 95:1-7a

JOY TO THE WORLD

Joy to the world, the Lord is come!
Let earth receive her King!
Let ev'ry heart prepare Him room,
And heav'n and nature sing,
And heav'n and nature sing,
And heav'n, and heav'n and nature sing.

Joy to the earth, the Savior reigns!
Let men their songs employ,
while fields and floods, rocks, hills, and plains
repeat the sounding joy,
repeat the sounding joy,
repeat, repeat the sounding joy.

No more let sins and sorrows grow,
nor thorns infest the ground;
He comes to make His blessings flow
far as the curse is found,
far as the curse is found,
far as, far as the curse is found.

He rules the world with truth and grace,
and makes the nations prove
the glories of His righteousness
and wonders of His love,
and wonders of His love,
and wonders, wonders of His love.

Isaac Watts (1719)

13
MY TURN

He makes me lie down in green pastures. He leads me beside
still waters, He restores my soul.

I wasn't used to it; being the recipient. I didn't like it; being the
rester, the observer, the sick. With cancer it seemed like so many
things around me were being done to me, for me or without me.
Grrr. I'm not fond of sitting around. So I didn't do it well. Mind
you, I am fond of a good nap, but I usually take a nap because I
fall asleep, then wake up and say, "Hey, good nap!" Intentional
rest was for someone else. Until it was my turn. Ahh, taking
turns: a childhood lesson that came back to haunt me. Could we
skip my turn? No. Could I not play that game? No. Did I have
to play alone? No.

———————

God was calling me to put my many cares into his
consistently capable and strong hands.

———————

Maybe it was my turn in a good way, in God's best way for me.
It was my turn to look to God to help me to sit when I wanted
to stand, to be calm when I wanted to clamber, to rest when I
wanted to run. He was always there with me, not chaining me to
the ground and forcing me to sit, but patting the sofa next to him
and beckoning me to come and relax. He was calling me to his
side to be engulfed in his embrace and to put my many cares into

his consistently capable and strong hands. There I rested, there I was stilled and there I was restored.

Read more of what God says to us ...

I lift up my eyes to the hills. From where does my help come? My help comes from the Lord, who made heaven and earth. He will not let your foot be moved; he who keeps you will not slumber. Behold, he who keeps Israel will neither slumber nor sleep.
PSALM 121:1-4

Sing for joy, O heavens, and exult, O earth; break forth, O mountains, into singing! For the Lord has comforted his people and will have compassion on his afflicted.
ISAIAH 49:13

WONDERFUL GRACE OF JESUS

Wonderful Grace of Jesus, greater than all my sin;
How shall my tongue describe it,
Where shall its praise begin?
Taking away my burden, setting my spirit free;
O the Wonderful Grace of Jesus reaches me!

Refrain
Wonderful the matchless Grace of Jesus,
Deeper than the mighty rolling sea;
Higher than the mountain, sparkling like a fountain,
All sufficient Grace for even me.
Broader than the scope of my transgressions,
Greater far than all my sin and shame
O magnify the precious name of Jesus,
PRAISE HIS NAME!

Wonderful Grace of Jesus, reaching to all the lost;
By it I have been pardoned, saved to the uttermost.
Chains have been torn asunder, giving me liberty;
O the Wonderful Grace of Jesus, reaches me! [*Refrain*]

Haidor Lillenas (1918)

14
TEMPTING

Humble yourselves, therefore, under the mighty hand of God so that at the proper time he may exalt you ...

1 PETER 5:6

I love getting credit. I love being acknowledged and complimented. If someone said, "You have done a great job," my head would swell. "You have such a positive attitude" ... more swelling. "You are handling this cancer so well" ... head swelling even more if that was possible. Oh, it was possible.

Don't get me wrong. I think encouragement is good for the soul, and God did and will continue to use it in my life. But when I am the recipient of encouraging words I need to know how to process them so that the encouragement along with my prideful nature doesn't clog up my avenues of worship and praise to God. Well meant and God sent compliments sometimes tempt me to sin.

Where does encouragement in the form of a compliment take you? To self-importance like it does me? To pridefulness? To self-incrimination as you consider all of the ways you don't measure up? You may experience all or none of these. Negative thoughts and feelings like these are rarely intentional. They seem to pop up from nowhere. Sometimes I feel like I'm mentally entrenched in these thoughts with no way to escape. But with God's spirit living in me I do have a way of escape as it says in the verse below (1 Corinthians 10:13).

It will happen. We will be tempted. Tempted to embrace and dwell in pervasive, entwining sins of the heart and mind like pride. Tempted to wallow in guilt about past sins long since confessed and forgiven. We will be tempted by a host of things. But our sweet and loving God doesn't just sit there and watch, he gives us a way of escape. And I'll take it.

Prayer: God please help me to recognize when my mental wheels are spinning in a way that doesn't bring honor to you. Whether it's the result of a compliment that I process wrongly or a result of my crazy brain doing a number on the peace of heart and mind that you offer me. When I'm drowning in these issues please help me to recognize it, repent of it and gladly take the holy hand of escape that you offer to me.

Read further …

> *No temptation has overtaken you that is not common to man.*
> *God is faithful, and he will not let you be tempted beyond your*
> *ability, but with the temptation he will also provide the way of*
> *escape, that you may be able to endure it.*
>
> 1 CORINTHIANS 10:13

TO GOD BE THE GLORY

To God be the glory, great things He hath done,
So loved He the world that He gave us His Son,
Who yielded His life an atonement for sin,
And opened the life gate that all may go in.

Refrain:
Praise the Lord, praise the Lord, let the earth hear His voice!
Praise the Lord, praise the Lord, let the people rejoice!
Oh, come to the Father, through Jesus the Son,
And give Him the glory, great things He hath done.

Oh, perfect redemption, the purchase of blood,
To every believer the promise of God;
The vilest offender who truly believes,
That moment from Jesus a pardon receives. [*Refrain*]

Great things He hath taught us, great things He hath done,
And great our rejoicing through Jesus the Son;
But purer, and higher, and greater will be
Our wonder, our transport, when Jesus we see. [*Refrain*]

Fanny Crosby (1875)

15
INVITING

Let each of us please his neighbor for his good, to build him up.

ROMANS 15:2

Some are inviters, some are the invited, and some are probably halfway in between. But I think most of us lean to one side or the other. It seems to me that sometimes the inviter needs to be invited. The includer, included. I guess that the invited are content to wait for their invitation. I often find myself in the discontent group.

So, how should I respond? Sit here and whine? ... lacks productivity and spiritual growth but is the easiest option by far. Or perhaps pray about my circumstance and my attitude.

Maybe, instead of focusing on being invited,
I should focus on being inviting.

God gives me his mercy because I'm in great need. I need to show that same mercy to others, no matter what my circumstances. God didn't stop using me because I was physically out of commission. I could pray for others, give them a phone call or invite them over for lunch, even if they needed to bring the lunch. I could be inviting.

Prayer: Lord, please help me to use the times that I find myself inactive and relatively alone to contemplate who and how you want me to be. I am so grateful for the love and attention so many people have shown me; so why do I long for still more attention from others? Please help me to be sensitive and thoughtful of others. Instead of focusing on my troubles, please help me to focus on you. May my life point to you.

More good news …

> *A new commandment I give to you, that you love one another: just as I have loved you, you also are to love one another. By this all people will know that you are my disciples, if you have love for one another.*
>
> JOHN 13:34-35

> *Then the King will say to those on his right, 'Come, you who are blessed by my Father, inherit the kingdom prepared for you from the foundation of the world. For I was hungry and you gave me food, I was thirsty and you gave me drink, I was a stranger and you welcomed me, I was naked and you clothed me, I was sick and you visited me, I was in prison and you came to me.' Then the righteous will answer him, saying, 'Lord, when did we see you hungry and feed you, or thirsty and give you drink? And when did we see you a stranger and welcome you, or naked and clothe you? And when did we see you sick or in prison and visit you?' And the King will answer them, 'Truly, I say to you, as you did it to one of the least of these my brothers, you did it to me.'*
>
> MATTHEW 25:34-40

MAY THE MIND OF CHRIST MY SAVIOR

May the mind of Christ, my Savior,
Live in me from day to day,
By His love and pow'r controlling
All I do and say.

May the Word of God dwell richly
In my heart from hour to hour,
So that all may see I triumph
Only through His pow'r.

May the peace of God my Father
Rule my life in everything,
That I may be calm to comfort
Sick and sorrowing.

May the love of Jesus fill me
As the waters fill the sea;
Him exalting, self abasing,
This is victory.

May I run the race before me,
Strong and brave to face the foe,
Looking only unto Jesus
As I onward go.

May His beauty rest upon me,
As I seek the lost to win,
And may they forget the channel,
Seeing only Him.

Kate Wilkinson (1925)

16
CALM

Do nothing from selfish ambition or conceit, but in humility count others more significant than yourselves. Let each of you look not only to his own interests, but also to the interests of others.

PHILIPPIANS 2:3-4

I was frustrated. It was only 8 a.m. and I was frustrated. I felt misunderstood. I was misunderstood. The surgeon sat down, looked me straight in the eye as we talked and then left the room with what seemed to me none of the information I had tried to communicate. And I was left with no answers other than "I know what you want." "How do you know what I want?" I grumbled to myself. "I don't even know what I want!" What do I do? Try to explain again? Write to him? Growl to my husband and friends? Pause? Quiet down? Calm myself? So many options, so little time.

Later that morning, as I was sitting in a coffee shop, I heard a man pointedly complaining about the service he had at a different restaurant. The server for his party couldn't remember what had been ordered by whom so he needed to ask this man's party … more than once. Now the man was complaining. He said that not only did the server confuse the orders, he also probably had dirty hands and was placing them wrongly around the patrons' water glasses. I was beginning to think that this guy shouldn't eat out!

Did the complainer think about his server? About the day he'd been having, the load he was carrying? Did I consider my surgeon and the burdens he bore? Why should we? (Great now I'm in kahoots with another whiner!) It was his dinner. It was my appointment. It was his water glass. It was my cancer. It was his lifestyle. It was my life.

The more I allow God's Spirit to flow through me and out of me to others, and the more I delight in him, the more my frustrations melt away.

As it turns out, it's not about him or me. It's about Jesus who gave his life, without complaints or conditions, to my undeserving self. He avails to me the calm, the quiet and the patience of his Spirit who lives within me. The irony is that the more I allow God's Spirit to flow through me and out of me to others, and the more I delight in him, the more my frustrations melt away.

God tells us in his word …

> *For my thoughts are not your thoughts, neither are your ways my ways, declares the Lord. For as the heavens are higher than the earth, so are my ways higher than your ways and my thoughts than your thoughts.*
>
> ISAIAH 55:8-9

see #3 in Afterwords page 105.

TAKE MY LIFE

Take my life and let it be
consecrated, Lord, to thee.
Take my moments and my days;
let them flow in ceaseless praise,
let them flow in ceaseless praise.

Take my hands and let them move
at the impulse of thy love.
Take my feet and let them be
swift and beautiful for thee,
swift and beautiful for thee.

Take my voice and let me sing
always, only, for my King.
Take my lips and let them be
filled with messages from thee,
filled with messages from thee.

Take my will and make it thine;
it shall be no longer mine.
Take my heart it is thine own;
it shall be thy royal throne,
it shall be thy royal throne.

Take my love; my Lord, I pour
at thy feet its treasure store.
Take myself, and I will be
ever, only, all for thee,
ever, only, all for thee.

Frances Ridley Havergal (1874)

17
SADNESS

*Why are you cast down, O my soul, and why are you in turmoil
within me? Hope in God; for I shall again praise him, my
salvation and my God.*

PSALM 42:5-6a

I was tired and sad that morning. No particular reason I can
come up with, just plain 'ole tired and plain 'ole sad. It was a
cancer-borne weariness resulting in lack of motivation, listless-
ness and despondency. Didn't like those feelings then, don't like
them now.

I'm a doer. (I mean that in a positive way, not in a "you need to
call the police" sort of way.) I like to accomplish things and be
with people. I guess you'd say I'm a task-oriented extrovert. So,
on that morning of quiet contemplation I found the quietness
very loud and my emotions in the dumps. But it's okay for me
to be sad. Not only that, but when I am down in the dumps Jesus
cares about me and for me as nobody else ever will, and he com-
forts me as nobody else ever can.

When your embrace seems to be all that there is,
please help me to remember that it is way more
than enough.

Sad is an emotion; it is not a sin. It can lead to sin as any emotion can. Anger can lead to hate. Fear or happiness can both lead to lack of trust. And sadness can lead to despair. But sadness alone is okay. We need to be aware of our bent to sinning while not letting the accuser of the saints pile on sin that is not there. We have enough real sin to deal with without adding on.

Prayer: Lord, please dry my tears if that's what's best, calm me and help me to trust you. Please help me to settle into your arms, warmed by your embrace. And when your embrace seems to be all that there is, please help me to remember that it is way more than enough.

Read more good news …

> *When the righteous cry for help, the Lord hears and delivers them out of all their troubles. The Lord is near to the brokenhearted and saves the crushed in spirit.*
>
> PSALM 34:17-18

LOVE DIVINE, ALL LOVES EXCELLING

Love divine, all loves excelling,
joy of heav'n, to earth come down,
fix in us Thy humble dwelling;
all Thy faithful mercies crown.
Jesus, Thou art all compassion;
pure, unbounded love Thou art;
visit us with Thy salvation; enter ev'ry trembling heart.

Breathe, O breathe Thy loving Spirit
into ev'ry troubled breast!
Let us all in Thee inherit; let us find the promised rest.
Take away our bent to sinning; Alpha and Omega be;
end of faith, as its beginning, set our hearts at liberty.

Come, Almighty, to deliver; let us all Thy life receive;
suddenly return and never, nevermore Thy temples leave.
Thee we would be always blessing,
serve Thee as Thy hosts above,
pray and praise Thee without ceasing,
glory in Thy perfect love.

Finish then Thy new creation; pure and spotless let us be.
Let us see Thy great salvation perfectly restored in Thee.
Changed from glory into glory,
till in heav'n we take our place,
till we cast our crowns before Thee,
lost in wonder, love, and praise.

Charles Wesley (1747)

18
FEAR

...casting all your anxieties on him, because he cares for you.

1 PETER 5:7

There is always something to be afraid of. Always. Real or imagined, thought provoking or adrenaline producing, fear is available to us. I'm afraid of cockroaches. I grew up in South Florida where they are big enough to tow your car. You can explain to me, as I can explain to you, that my fear is unwarranted, unnecessary and silly. Duly noted, but nevertheless roaches give me the heebie-jeebies.

I realize my example is trite compared to significant concerns that people face every day ... like having cancer. But I choose that example because in God's economy being afraid of anything is as unnecessary as being afraid of a cockroach. In the economy of this world many things can hurt us, and they do. Many things are fear producing. We pray against those things happening in our lives and in the lives of others. We ask fervently for those things to end and to be removed from our lives, as we should. We are invited to do that. "Cast all your cares upon him as he cares for you" (1 Peter 5:7). Even Jesus asked his father to take away his impending earthly death.

We are not asked to get over our fears but we are asked to give over our fears. Give them to the one who is higher than we are. The one who sees the big picture. The one who loves us perfectly. And "... perfect loves casts out fear" (1 John 4:18).

We are not asked to get over our fears but we are asked to give over our fears.

For more insight from God's word...

> *I will bless the Lord at all times; his praise shall continually be in my mouth. My soul makes its boast in the Lord; let the humble hear and be glad. Oh, magnify the Lord with me, and let us exalt his name together! I sought the Lord, and he answered me and delivered me from all my fears.*

PSALM 34:1-4

LEANING ON THE EVERLASTING ARMS

What a fellowship, what a joy divine,
leaning on the everlasting arms;
what a blessedness, what a peace is mine,
leaning on the everlasting arms.

Refrain:
Leaning, leaning,
safe and secure from all alarms;
leaning, leaning,
leaning on the everlasting arms.

O how sweet to walk in this pilgrim way,
leaning on the everlasting arms;
O how bright the path grows from day to day,
leaning on the everlasting arms. [*Refrain*]

What have I to dread, what have I to fear,
leaning on the everlasting arms?
I have blessed peace with my Lord so near,
leaning on the everlasting arms. [*Refrain*]

E. A. Hoffman (1887)

19
MOURNING

*Rejoice in hope, be patient in tribulation, be constant in prayer
... Rejoice with those who rejoice, weep with those who weep.*

ROMANS 12:12 &15

Have you heard the song of a mourning dove? It's a sad but beautiful tune. Maybe that's what God hears from us when we mourn. During my cancer I was mourning for things I was losing and things I might lose. I was wrangling with a disease that caused me to be in dire circumstances. A disease that tripped me up when I was minding my own business. I didn't see it coming and I didn't know where it was going or if it would take me with it. So I mourned.

We all mourn sometimes and we should. Mourning happens to everyone. It's as much a part of our lives as is laughing, crying, praising and praying. We mourn.

God, and only he, through his infinite
knowledge, grace and love toward us
can give us mourning and hope
all mixed and mingled together.

We all experience losses both big and small. Sometimes we experience temporary loss and sometimes what we would deem the ultimate loss. It is fine and even healthy to mourn those losses.

But the good news is that we can mourn without losing hope. With Jesus dwelling in us we always have hope. So, invite him to indwell your life if you haven't already. If you are his child, allow his presence in you to bless you with the hope only he can give.

God, and only he, through his infinite knowledge, grace and love toward us can give us mourning and hope all mixed and mingled together.

God tells us in his word ...

> *But we do not want you to be uninformed, brothers, about those who are asleep, that you may not grieve as others do who have no hope. For since we believe that Jesus died and rose again, even so, through Jesus, God will bring with him those who have fallen asleep.*
>
> 1 THESSALONIANS 4:13-14

TURN YOUR EYES UPON JESUS

O soul, are you weary and troubled?
No light in the darkness you see?
There's light for a look at the Savior,
And life more abundant and free!

Refrain:
Turn your eyes upon Jesus,
Look full in His wonderful face,
And the things of earth will grow strangely dim,
In the light of His glory and grace.

Through death into life everlasting
He passed, and we follow Him there;
O'er us sin no more hath dominion—
For more than conqu'rors we are! [*Refrain*]

His Word shall not fail you—He promised;
Believe Him, and all will be well:
Then go to a world that is dying,
His perfect salvation to tell! [*Refrain*]

Helen Howarth Lemmel (1922)

20
TEARS

You have ... put my tears into Your bottle;
Are they not in Your book?

PSALM 56:8

I had cancer for crying out loud, which I do on numerous occasions; cry out loud that is. It's hard to be around me ... even for me! I never know when a gasket of tears is going to burst and I imagine that onlookers might be thinking, "Oh no. There she goes again!"

Truth be told, I don't want to cry. Crying just happens to me and at the most inopportune times .... Like the time I was in a breakfast shop journaling on my computer. I was sitting in a booth facing a man who didn't know me from Adam's house cat. Tears were running down my cheeks as a result of an encouraging text someone had sent me. The guy facing me didn't know me and now probably doesn't want to; no wonder!

My Heavenly Father calms my fears, allows my tears and dries them with his hand.

But I'm learning not to be embarrassed and apologetic about my tears. God created me. He created my tears and he created them to fall. And so they do; to lovely hymns telling me truth after truth about my Savior, to a memory of a childhood moment of pure glee, to the expertly crafted pages of a book I'm reading, to a wish to be with my children one and all, to memories of their childhood often squandered by me and long since gone. I think many thoughts and cry many tears both happy and sad, a big giant combo of dampness. And deep, deep inside, I wonder how much time I have left for tears to fall. And deeper still than that, I know that all is right because God is my Father. He calms my fears, allows my tears and dries them with his hand.

I was sad, but not without hope. I was lonesome, but never alone. I was despondent, but comforted. I was happy and brimming with glee. I am allowed to shed tears of all kinds, because I am an image bearer and shedding tears is one image of our Savior.

Prayer: Thank you Lord for the ability to experience, to think, to remember, to ask forgiveness, to forgive, to laugh and to cry. It is all glorious, as are you and the peace you bring.

Read more ...

> *Peace I leave with you; my peace I give to you. Not as the world gives do I give to you. Let not your hearts be troubled, neither let them be afraid.*
>
> JOHN 14:27

LIKE A RIVER GLORIOUS

Like a river glorious is God's perfect peace,
over all victorious in its bright increase:
perfect, yet it floweth fuller every day;
perfect, yet it groweth deeper all the way.

Refrain:
Stayed upon Jehovah, hearts are fully blest,
finding, as he promised, perfect peace and rest.

Hidden in the hollow of his blessed hand,
Never foe can follow, never traitor stand.
Not a surge of worry, not a shade of care
Not a blast of hurry touch the spirit there. [*Refrain*]

Every joy or trial falleth from above,
Traced upon our dial by the Sun of Love;
We may trust Him fully all for us to do;
They who trust Him wholly find Him wholly true. [*Refrain*]

Frances Ridley Havergal (1876)

21
PRAYER

*Do not be anxious about anything, but in everything by prayer
and supplication with thanksgiving let your requests be made
known to God. And the peace of God, which surpasses all
understanding, will guard your hearts and your minds in
Christ Jesus.*

PHILIPPIANS 4:6-7

Many people prayed for me during my walk through my cancer.
They offered to pray. I asked them to pray. I know they did pray.
I prayed. Praying was done. Another thing I know is that God
heard our prayers. Isaiah 65:24 says, "Before they call I will answer; while they are yet speaking I will hear."

Many things were prayed for. There were prayers for me, my
family, our trust in God. The list was long. As you might imagine
the foremost request was that God would remove my cancer
from me without chemo, surgery or any treatment. I wanted my
cancer to be gone immediately and with no lingering fears. I
prayed that it would leave my body and I had no doubt that God
could do that in an instant. If he is really God, he can do whatever he chooses. He answered many of our prayers in the affirm-
ative but the answer to that single prayer was "No." And that
answer was okay. Why? Because the best prayer that any of us
can pray is what Jesus prayed before his crucifixion, "God, your
will be done." Jesus said, "Father, if you are willing, remove this
cup from me. Nevertheless, not my will, but yours, be done"
(Luke 22:42).

As I prayed and pray still, I'm reminded that God knows all that there is to know and he loves me more than I can ever imagine. If God knows everything then he knows what's best for me.

The best prayer that any of us can pray is "God, your will be done."

So my prayer was and still is that by God's grace I'll take whatever this cancer brings and that God will use it for his glory. That he will use it in my life and the lives of those around me however he chooses. That this part of my story will be intertwined with his glory and grace. God's will be done.

More about prayer from God's word …

> *Likewise the Spirit helps us in our weakness. For we do not know what to pray for as we ought, but the Spirit himself intercedes for us with groanings too deep for words. And he who searches hearts knows what is the mind of the Spirit, because the Spirit intercedes for the saints according to the will of God. And we know that for those who love God all things work together for good for those who are called according to his purpose.*
> ROMANS 8:26-28

HAVE THINE OWN WAY LORD

Have thine own way, Lord! Have thine own way!
Thou art the potter, I am the clay.
Mold me and make me after thy will,
while I am waiting, yielded and still.

Have thine own way, Lord! Have thine own way!
Search me and try me, Savior today!
Wash me just now, Lord, wash me just now,
as in thy presence humbly I bow.

Have thine own way, Lord! Have thine own way!
Wounded and weary, help me I pray!
Power, all power, surely is thine!
Touch me and heal me, Savior divine!

Have thine own way, Lord! Have thine own way!
Hold o'er my being absolute sway.
Fill with thy Spirit till all shall see
Christ only, always, living in me!

Adelaide A. Pollard (1906)

22
DESERTER

*Your eyes saw my unformed substance; in your book were
written, every one of them, the days that were formed for me,
when as yet there was none of them.*

PSALM 139:16

I'm not a deserter. I don't quit in the middle of a game because I think I'm going to lose. I don't fail to show up for commitments I've made or leave in the middle of a job I'm doing. It's not nice. It's bad form. It's wrong. I don't want it to happen to me so I don't want to cause it for somebody else. Wow! Am I saintly or what? Don't answer that.

My feelings about not ditching out on folks are what fuel my distaste for dying; well, one of my distastes for it. I hate the thought of dropping out on people who, I've gotten the impression right or wrong, might need me or at the least be sorry that I'm not around. I hate to hurt people's feelings. I'm such a people pleaser.

The bottom line is I don't want to be responsible for taking someone away from someone else. It will happen eventually one way or the other. I prefer to opt for 'the other'. It's an ominous responsibility and I don't want it. The best news is, I don't have it.

God is in control. And as a believer I have full assurance that he knows what is best not only for me, but for those around me. He has charge of the number of my days and I have no doubt he's chosen the right number. I can rest in that knowledge and resting always sounds good to me.

As a believer I have full assurance that God knows what is best not only for me, but for those around me.

Learn more from God's word ...

> *Let not your hearts be troubled. Believe in God; believe also in me. In my Father's house are many rooms. If it were not so, would I have told you that I go to prepare a place for you? And if I go and prepare a place for you, I will come again and will take you to myself, that where I am you may be also.*
>
> JOHN 14:1-3

See #4 in Afterwords page 105.

WHEN WE ALL GET TO HEAVEN

Sing the wondrous love of Jesus,
sing his mercy and his grace;
in the mansions bright and blessed
he'll prepare for us a place.

Refrain:
When we all get to heaven,
what a day of rejoicing that will be!
When we all see Jesus
we'll sing and shout the victory.

While we walk the pilgrim pathway
clouds will overspread the sky,
but when traveling days are over,
not a shadow, not a sigh. [*Refrain*]

Let us then be true and faithful,
trusting, serving every day;
just one glimpse of Him in glory
will the toils of life repay. [*Refrain*]

E. E. Hewitt (1898)

23
PERSPECTIVE

*So we do not lose heart. Though our outer self is wasting away,
our inner self is being renewed day by day. For this light
momentary affliction is preparing for us an eternal weight of
glory beyond all comparison, as we look not to the things that
are seen but to the things that are unseen. For the things that
are seen are transient, but the things that are unseen are eternal.*

2 CORINTHIANS 4:16-18

Gazing out of large picture windows into a lush forest in North Florida, the calm was engulfing. It's always nice to get a different view out of a different window. It is also nice to enjoy that view with people you love. I was midway through my cancer treatments and we were visiting my sister and her husband.

During our visit we made a trip to a local art gallery. The artwork was alluring. So much to see, so little time. I viewed the paintings, looking at some and studying others. Some paintings I barely noticed but others I gazed at, considering them from various angles. One of my favorite things to do is stand back from a painting to take in the entire work and then walk up very close to get a good look at the minute details.

————————

Nuanced and subtle, bold and forceful all mixed together by the ultimate artist, God presents himself to us through his word.

————————

Taking in the artwork reminded me of taking in my cancer. I was getting a closer look at cancer than I'd had before; closer than I'd ever wanted. I'd become intimately acquainted with many angles of the disease. And through it all God gave me an unerring resource for that journey, the resource of his word. His masterpiece laid out for us in print, voice and song.

Like the forest out my sister's window and the art in the museum, God's word is multifaceted. Sometimes parts of it slip by unnoticed while other parts grab our attention. Layer upon layer of leaves and sunlight, layer upon layer of paint, layer upon layer of truth. Nuanced and subtle, bold and forceful all mixed together by the ultimate artist, God presents himself to us through his word.

Read God's word...

> *Make a joyful noise to the Lord, all the earth! Serve the Lord with gladness! Come into his presence with singing! Know that the Lord, he is God! It is he who made us, and we are his; we are his people, and the sheep of his pasture. Enter his gates with thanksgiving, and his courts with praise! Give thanks to him; bless his name! For the Lord is good; his steadfast love endures forever, and his faithfulness to all generations.*
> PSALM 100

FOR THE BEAUTY OF THE EARTH

For the beauty of the earth,
for the glory of the skies,
for the love which from our birth
over and around us lies.

Refrain:
Lord of all, to Thee we raise
this, our hymn of grateful praise.

For the wonder of each hour
of the day and of the night,
hill and vale and tree and flower,
sun and moon and stars of light, [*Refrain*]

For the joy of human love,
brother, sister, parent, child,
friends on earth, and friends above,
for all gentle thoughts and mild, [*Refrain*]

For Thy-self, best gift divine,
to the world so freely given,
for that great, great love of Thine,
peace on earth and joy in heaven. [*Refrain*]

Folliott Sandford Pierpoint (1864)

24
GIVING SPACE

Trust in the Lord with all your heart, and do not lean on your own understanding. In all your ways acknowledge him, and he will make straight your paths.

PROVERBS 3:5-6

So many people stood by me during my walk through cancer. But none were more present than the ones I love the most. This may not be the experience of everyone but it was mine and I am grateful for it, for them. God used my husband and my other family members both near and far to bolster me with unequaled love and support. My husband especially was watchful, available and loving. He was present. He was a godsend. Still is.

Sitting at the table after dinner has always been our time. Throughout the years of our marriage it's been our opportunity to relax and rehash our day. Some days seem to need more hashing than others. More often than not my husband Paul was the listener, I was the talker. No surprise there. Listening is a gift he has consistently given to me throughout our marriage and all the more during the time I was battling cancer.

During that time he carried his own unique burdens. I wasn't the only one with cancer. He 'had' cancer too. Day and night it was in his face. He prayed, he helped, he comforted and consoled. He did those things and more, above and beyond. He did everything he could to make it better but he could do nothing to make it go away. How frustrating that must have been.

Sometimes I prayed Lord, please help me to give my loved ones some space and some grace. Some space and grace to be cranky, solemn, talkative, happy, quiet, different. Different than they have been before.

My cancer was a wave that broke over my life, spilled into my husband's and rippled into the lives of others. And I have it on good authority that God doesn't waste water. My hope is to look back along with my loved ones on our unique experience as a time of God's healing and grace for all of us; a time to rejoice together in the peace and hope our Savior brings even in the middle of a storm.

Our Savior brings peace and hope even in the middle of a storm.

Learn more from God's word…

Therefore, since we have been justified by faith, we have peace with God through our Lord Jesus Christ. Through him we have also obtained access by faith into this grace in which we stand, and we rejoice in hope of the glory of God. Not only that, but we rejoice in our sufferings, knowing that suffering produces endurance, and endurance produces character, and character produces hope, and hope does not put us to shame, because God's love has been poured into our hearts through the Holy Spirit who has been given to us.
ROMANS 5:1-5

MASTER, THE TEMPEST IS RAGING

Master, the tempest is raging!
The billows are tossing high!
The sky is o'ershadowed with blackness,
No shelter or help is nigh:
Carest Thou not that we perish?
How canst Thou lie asleep,
When each moment so madly is threat'ning
A grave in the angry deep?

The winds and the waves shall obey Thy will.
Peace, be still! Peace, be still!
Whether the wrath of the storm-tossed sea,
Or demons, or men, or whatever it be,
No water can swallow the ship where lies
the Master of ocean and earth and skies;
They all shall sweetly obey Thy will!
Peace, be still! Peace, be still!
They all shall sweetly obey Thy will!
Peace, Peace, be still!

Mary Ann Baker (1874)

25
WHAT IF ?

I have been crucified with Christ. It is no longer I who live, but Christ who lives in me. And the life I now live in the flesh I live by faith in the Son of God, who loved me and gave himself for me.

GALATIANS 2:20

A strange thing has happened to me. My cancer appears to be gone and my gratitude for that is inexpressible. But now, during this time when it seems logical for me to walk away from this experience and move back into my pre-cancerous modes, I sometimes feel more stymied than earlier when I was in the midst of battle. There is a trepidation within me. A fear that I can, and might be, snuck up on again.

Maybe I'm experiencing some kind of post-traumatic stress; cancer was traumatic and I now I'm stressed. When you find yourself in the middle of a battle you follow the prescribed steps to conquer the foe. It's like experiencing some more common trauma which you handle with calmness and control and then when it's all over you proceed to fall apart. I'm not a fan of falling apart.

God is the one who can keep the enemy from using the 'what ifs' in my life to rob me of 'what is'.

Now I'm wary. I'm proceeding with a little more caution than I once had. During this period of cautious emergence into my new normal, I don't want wary to become worried. I don't want stressed to become scared or stymied to become stopped. What if my cancer returns? How will things go if I meet this giant again? What will happen? The same thing that happened before … God will be there. He will walk with me then as he has so many times in the past. He is a constant. He is the one who can keep the enemy from using the 'what ifs' in my life to rob me of 'what is'. The 'what is', is Jesus Christ crucified, who died to pay for my sins and now abides in me. And that 'what is' is far greater than any 'what if'.

We can't help concerns that sneak up on us, like cancer snuck up on me not too long ago. So here I am again, placing my new struggles and concerns into the capable hands of my Father in heaven. There will always be something to catch me unawares and bring me to my knees before him, which is right where I belong.

Reflect on this …

> *Rejoice always, pray without ceasing, give thanks in all circumstances; for this is the will of God in Christ Jesus for you.*
> 1 THESSALONIANS 5:16-18

TRUST AND OBEY

When we walk with the Lord
in the light of his word,
what a glory he sheds on our way!
While we do his good will,
he abides with us still,
and with all who will trust and obey.

Refrain:
Trust and obey, for there's no other way
to be happy in Jesus, but to trust and obey.

Not a burden we bear,
not a sorrow we share,
but our toil he doth richly repay;
not a grief or a loss,
not a frown or a cross,
but is blest if we trust and obey. [*Refrain*]

But we never can prove
the delights of his love
until all on the altar we lay;
for the favor he shows,
for the joy he bestows,
are for them who will trust and obey. [*Refrain*]

Then in fellowship sweet
we will sit at his feet,
or we'll walk by his side in the way;
what he says we will do,
where he sends we will go;
never fear, only trust and obey. [*Refrain*]

John H. Sammis (1887)

26
PROMISES

God is not man, that he should lie, or a son of man, that he should change his mind. Has he said, and will he not do it? Or has he spoken, and will he not fulfill it?

NUMBERS 23:19

There are no promises, not in this life anyway. I'm sitting here writing my thoughts about a cancer that at this time seems to be gone. It was a very aggressive type and there is no promise that it will never return someplace else in my body. Some may be reading this who know that their cancer will never go away. It's here to stay and be dealt with. Others may have lost a loved one to cancer or another disease that refused to relinquish its hold.

It's easy in times of trouble to look to people and other solutions for things, but some promises in this life are just not there. There may be momentary success, even victory over a piece of this puzzle called life. But there is no hope in looking sideways for ultimate solutions. That's why God calls us to look up. That's where the true promise lies. The hope, the glory, and the peace all come from above. They come from him.

Sometimes even when we look up, our view seems blocked. The clouds of doubt blur our vision, the winds that blow cause tears to run down our cheeks, but our focus needs to be far beyond those obstructions. The clouds will part and our vision will clear to see the only one who can, as my oncologist said to me, "get you through this."

I want to be taken through whatever my challenges are by the true promise-bearer. He gave his Son to me when I was undeserving. He promises me a place in his kingdom and eternal life to enjoy with him. He makes that promise to everyone who will bow a knee to him and ask him in. He will enter our hearts. And even beyond that, God does a work in us to bring us to the point of making the step to ask him in. The promise is sure.

I want to be taken through whatever my challenges are by the true promise-bearer.

Read God's word ...

For when God made a promise to Abraham, since he had no one greater by whom to swear, he swore by himself, saying, "Surely I will bless you and multiply you." And thus Abraham, having patiently waited, obtained the promise. ... So when God desired to show more convincingly to the heirs of the promise the unchangeable character of his purpose, he guaranteed it with an oath, so that by two unchangeable things, in which it is impossible for God to lie, we who have fled for refuge might have strong encouragement to hold fast to the hope set before us.

HEBREWS 6:13-15,17-18

Behold, I stand at the door and knock. If anyone hears my voice and opens the door, I will come in to him and eat with him, and he with me.

REVELATION 3:20

STANDING ON THE PROMISES

Standing on the promises of Christ my king,
through eternal ages let his praises ring;
glory in the highest, I will shout and sing,
standing on the promises of God.

Refrain:
Standing, standing,
standing on the promises of God my Savior;
standing, standing,
I'm standing on the promises of God.

Standing on the promises that cannot fail,
when the howling storms of doubt and fear assail,
by the living Word of God I shall prevail,
standing on the promises of God. [*Refrain*]

Standing on the promises of Christ the Lord,
bound to him eternally by love's strong cord,
overcoming daily with the Spirit's sword,
standing on the promises of God. [*Refrain*]

Standing on the promises I cannot fall,
listening every moment to the Spirit's call,
resting in my Savior as my all in all,
standing on the promises of God. [*Refrain*]

Russell Kelso Carter (1886)

AFTERWORDS

Here are some things I learned:

1. God has and will continue to use my experience with cancer for good in my life.

2. I don't like to ask for help and I think that's true of many of us.

    I think I should be independent … God made me dependent.

    I don't want to impose on others … God put us here for each other.

    I don't even want to need help … that ship has sailed. We all need help at one time or another.

    I often needed to specify about what I needed. That's not only okay, it's good and helpful to those helping us.

    When I allowed someone to help me I was helping them in return. It's a win-win. It's the church at it's best.

3. Trusting my doctors was important. I prayed for the best doctors for me during the course of my cancer treatment. I believe that God provided just that. I asked very many questions of my doctors. There is no stupid question. I think it's important to get all of your questions answered. But at some point I needed to put my trust in my doctors and their knowledge and abilities.

4. My desire to stay alive, not just for myself but for others, strongly motivated me to faithfully go through the entire cancer treatment regardless of how unpalatable it was.

INDEXES
LIST OF SCRIPTURE AND HYMNS
BY CHAPTER

SCRIPTURES
OLD TESTAMENT

NEW TESTAMENT

HYMNS

ABOUT THE AUTHOR

Carol Frey is blessed with a wonderful family. She is happily married to her patient husband Paul, has three grown and married children and eight grandchildren. Back in the dark ages, before she was married, she obtained a BS in Special Education from Auburn University. Her college days were also the time when she began leading Bible studies for women. She is a freelance writer and also the author of three other books; two cookbooks and one children's party book. Carol was a speaker for Stonecroft ministries throughout the Southeast from 2009-2016, when that was interrupted by an appointment with cancer.

Follow Carol on Facebook:

www.Facebook.com/carolfreyauthor

There you will find, among other things, a link to purchase all of her books.

CPSIA information can be obtained
at www.ICGtesting.com
Printed in the USA
LVHW051509031119
636188LV00008B/157/P

9 781690 828006